HANBO-JUTSU
USE OF THE HANBO, WALKING
STICK AND BATON FOR SELF-DEFENSE

BY

Joseph J. Truncale

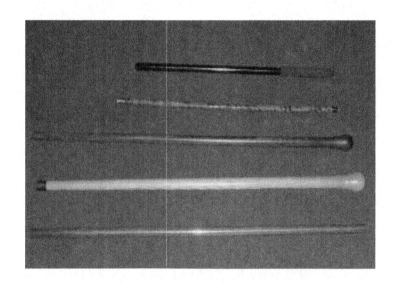

HANBO-JUTSU
USE OF THE HANBO, CANE, WALKING STICK AND BATON FOR SELF-DEFENSE

BY

Joseph J. Truncale

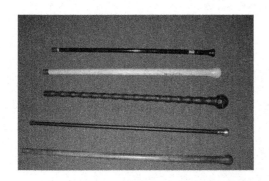

Copyright © 2015 Joseph J. Truncale Completely Revised.

No portion of this next may be copied in any way without permission from the author and /or publisher of this text.

WARNING

The information, techniques and tactics in this text could result in serious injury or death. The author, publisher, instructor and distributor of this text disclaim any liability or injuries of any type that the reader may incur from the use of such information. It is the reader's responsibility to research and comply with all local, state, and federal laws and regulations concerning the possession, carry and use of any type of self-defense weapon. This manual is for academic study only.

TABLE OF CONTENTS

Introduction: Hanbo-Jutsu, the cane and walking stick:........4

Chapter 1: Nomenclature of staffs/canes/ walking sticks:.....6
Chapter 2: Balance, Stance and Movement:........................10

Chapter 3: Basic Methods to Grip the Hanbo/cane/stick:......13
Chapter 4: Basic Self-Defense Principles & Force Factors:..17

Chapter 5: Vulnerable Areas & Natural body weapons:........20
Chapter 6: Blocking methods using the Hanbo,cane,stick:..22

Chapter 7: Basic Striking Techniques:...............................29
Chapter 8: Hanbo, Baton Control & Takedowns:..................41

Chapter 9: Punching Attack Counters:................................45
Chapter 10: Kicking Attack Counters:................................48

Chapter 11: Choke Attack Counters:..................................50
Chapter 12: Stick and Wrist Grab Hug Counters:.................52

Chapter 13. Bear Hug Counters:..54
Chapter 14: Knife Attack Counters:...................................56

Conclusion and Summary:..59

References and recommended material:................................60
About the Author:..63
Books, manuals and guides by the author:............................65
Special Thanks:..69

INTRODUCTION

HANBO-JUTSU, THE CANE, STICK AND BATON

The stick as a self-defense weapon has been around since the dawn of humankind. The first time early man picked up a stick and used it against an enemy may have been the beginning of weapon warfare. The beauty of the staff is that any length of stick can be employed as an effective self-defense tool. Most people relate the formal use of the staff, whether a Bo, Jo, Hanbo, Cane, Walking Stick and baton to the Asian martial arts. However, staff techniques for combat and self-defense were also developed to a high degree of sophistication in European countries as well.

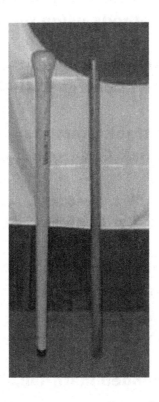

In many countries formal weapons were outlawed or restricted to only those in the military. However, the walking staff was a practical tool for the average citizen to have in most societies. Sophisticated techniques and tactics were developed using the staff, most of which came from the spear and sword techniques of the military. One of the great things about the staff is that it can be used in such a wide variety of ways. The techniques and tactics of the Bo, Jo and Hanbo were developed originally to counter sword and other weapon attacks. Though they are often taught as a weapon against weapon tool, the techniques can also be used against unarmed attacks. In fact, the advantage of learning the Hanbo is that the very same techniques and tactics can relate directly to the use of the standard cane, walking stick or even the police baton.

This book will focus on the use of the Hanbo, hooked cane, walking stick and straight police baton. The illustrations will include examples of how to use the Hanbo, cane, walking stick and police baton. The length of the Hanbo is thirty six inches, which is the same as most canes and walking sticks. The only real difference is the diameter, which can vary in certain staff type weapons. The traditional Hanbo is about 3 ½ inches in diameter. The traditional walking stick like Cold Steel's Walkabout is about 4 ½ inches in diameter. The standard straight baton is about 26 inches in length and around one to two inches in diameter.

This is not a an all encompassing text on the use of the Hanbo, cane, walking stick and baton, as it would take several volumes to show all the techniques and variations of using the staff as a self-defense tool. This manual will show all the basic techniques of using the Hanbo, cane, walking stick and baton stick. It will also cover how to defend yourself using the Hanbo, cane and stick to counter most types of attacks. It is hoped this manual encourages martial art and self-defense students to train and seek more knowledge in the use of the Hanbo, cane, walking stick and baton.

Joseph J. Truncale: Soke: Bushi Satori Ryu
February 25, 2008
Completely Revised: 2015 Joseph J. Truncale

CHAPTER 1

NOMENCLATURE OF STAFFS, CANES AND STICKS:

The type of wood used for staffs can vary, but they are almost always made from one of the harder woods such as red or white oak. In our modern age, you might see the Bo made from plastic at tournaments. For traditional use, the wood staff is used in training halls. The diameter of the Bo, Jo and Hanbo can vary between 3 ½ to 4 inches. The length can also vary, but in general, a Bo is around 6 feet in length (1.8288 meters), the Jo is around 4 feet in length (1.2192 meters), and the Hanbo is around 3 feet in length (0.9144 meters).

THE BO (6 Feet) THE JO (4 Feet) THE HANBO (3 Feet)

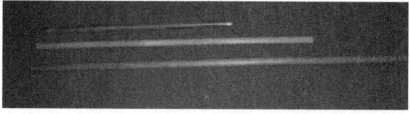

In general all staffs consist of **FIVE AREAS.** They are the middle portion, left side portion, right side portion, left side end and right side end. These are important to know when using the Hanbo.

The beauty of the Hanbo is that most of the techniques can also be used with a shorter staff or stick such as the 24 and 26 inch police batons and shorter canes or walking sticks. Unlike the Bo or Jo, the Hanbo is the most practical staff to learn because it can easily be carried legally and used as a walking stick. The Bo techniques often relate directly to the use of the Yari (spear) and the Naginata (sword/spear). The photographs show the relationship between the Hanbo and cane/walking stick that can be used for self-defense.

1. 26 Inch Straight Police Baton
2. 26 Inch Arnis Stick
3. 36 Inch Redwood Walking Stick
4. 36 Inch Walkabout XL from the Big Stick Company
5. 36 Inch Red Oak Traditional Hanbo
6. Various types of Canes (36 inch).

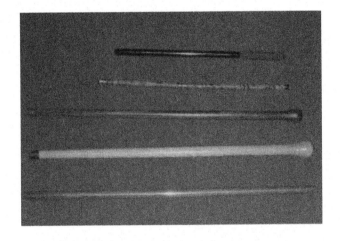

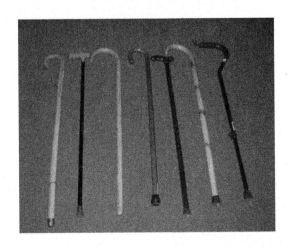

WALKING STICK/CANE NOMENCLATURE AND METHODS TO CARRY THE WALKING STICK/CANE

NOMENCLATURE:

There are several nomenclature terms used by different cane and walking stick systems. Bushi Satori Ryu uses the following terms for these two walking tools. The only difference between a cane and a walking stick is the cane will have a hook or handle that sticks out. The walking stick is straight with no hook or handle on it.

There are four basic parts of the cane and walking stick. (Note: Differences in the nomenclature of the cane and the standard walking stick).

The Cane Nomenclature: Length: 36 inches but can vary in cane length.

1. The Hook   (This is the handle of the cane)
2. The Hook Tip   (This is the tip portion on the handle of the cane)
3. The Shaft   (Also called the Long Portion)
4. The Tip (Also called the Long Portion Tip) portion.

The Walking Stick Nomenclature: Length: Usually about 36 inches in length.

1. Grip End   (This is the top of the stick on the grip portion)
2. Grip Portion (This is the portion where you would grip the stick)
3. Long Portion (This is the middle portion of the stick)
4. End Tip   (This is the tip or end portion of the stick)

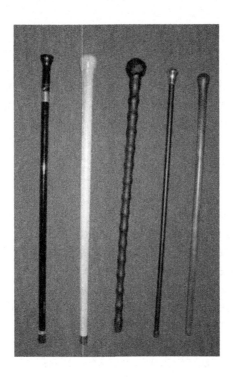

CHAPTER 2

BALANCE, STANCE AND MOVEMENT:

It does not matter which martial art you may practice, the first thing that is usually taught to students is stance, balance and movement. If you do not have this basic foundation, you may never be an effective martial artist. The following are the basic principles followed in most martial art systems.

BALANCE:

In Judo and Jujitsu, students are taught the basic eight points of balance. Understanding these eight points will help you to keep your own balance, as well as forcing your attacker off balance. Keep in mind that balance is a fluid concept. In other words, changing your foot and body position will also change your balance points. Every time you take a step your balance point also changes.

The eight basic balance points:
1. Forward balance point
2. Rear balance point
3. Left Side balance point
4. Right Side balance point
5. Forward Right 45 degree angle balance point
6. Forward Left 45 degree angle balance point
7. Rear Left 45 degree angle balance point
8. Rear Left 45 degree angle balance point

Important Note: If one uses a cane or walking stick because of balance problems, you can also perform the exercises and self-defense moves from a seated position. For those who cannot stand without a cane, but desire to use the cane for self-defense, consider using two canes when walking. This way one can be used to control your balance and the other cane can be used for self-defense.

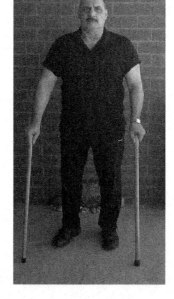

STANCE:

Different martial arts use various types of stances depending on the situation. The argument often heard by so called modern self-defense systems is that one should not worry about stance and you should be able to defend yourself from any position. The first part of the argument is false but the second part is true. The fact is, by understanding balance, you will automatically position yourself in the best possible position to defend yourself. That is called stance. There are numerous stances if you include all the variations, but for the purposes of this manual, we are only going to cover three basic stances that are used in learning the Hanbo, cane, walking stick and police baton. They are as follows:

1. Natural Open Leg Stance (Hachiji Dachi) This is a relaxed but ready position. The legs are about shoulder width apart and evenly distributed.

2. Front Stance (Zenkutsu Dachi) this is a very strong stance with the front leg bent forward almost over the front toe and the rear leg slightly bent. For practical use in self-defense, one does not have to have as deep a stance as the one shown in this photograph.

3. Straddle Leg Stance (Kiba Dachi – Horse Stance) The straddle leg stance is done with both legs a little further than shoulder width apart. Both legs are bent evenly for balance. This is a high straddle leg stance which is more practical for self-defense. You will often see a much deeper straddle leg stance in most styles of karate.

1.

2.

3.

BODY MOVEMENT AND SHIFTING:

Fighting and self-defense are not static activities. Stance, balance and movement are all related to each other. One has to be able to move when facing an opponent or an enemy who is attacking you. There are numerous patterns of movement taught in the martial arts, depending on the system being studied. Some modern martial art systems employ ten or more different body shifting methods, but for the purposes of this manual, we will only cover six ways to move.

1. **Forward Shuffle:** From the front stance position, move your lead foot forward about 12 inches followed by your rear foot. Always maintain your legs at shoulder width apart when moving. You should end up in a balanced front stance position.
2. **Rear Shuffle:** From the front stance position, move your rear foot back about 12 inches followed by your front foot. Always maintain your legs shoulder width apart. You should end up in a balanced front stance position.
3. **Left Side Step:** From the front stance position, move your left foot to the left side about 11 inches followed by your right foot as you end up in the front stance position.
4. **Right Side Step:** From the front stance position, move your right foot the right about 11 inches followed by your left foot as you end up in the front stance position.
5. **Forward Pivot:** From the front stance position, take a full step forward with your rear foot. You should end up in the front stance with your rear leg now forward. If you begin with your left leg forward, you will now have your right leg forward. If you begin with your right leg forward, you will now have your left leg forward.
6. **Rear Pivot:** From the front stance position, take a full step backward with your lead foot. You should end up in the front stance with your front foot now to the rear. If you begin with your left leg forward, you will now have your right foot forward. If you begin with your right leg forward, you will now have your left leg forward.

NOTE: There are numerous variations and angles one can employ after learning the above basic six patterns of movement.

CHAPTER 3

BASIC HANBO, CANE, STICK, BATON CARRY

AND GRIPPING TECHNIQUES

There are numerous ways to grip and carry the Hanbo, cane and walking stick depending on the techniques being used. If you desire to become skillful using the Hanbo, you should master all these carries and grips. Once you have learned these carries and grips, you should practice changing from one type of carry and grip to another until it is a fluid motion and you feel comfortable performing each technique.

1. Natural stance with the Hanbo next to you in either the right or left hand. There are two ways to grip the Hanbo in this position. (1) Your hand on top of the end. (2) Your hand gripping the portion of the Hanbo near the top.

1.

2.

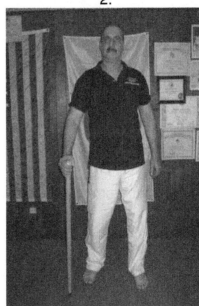

METHODS TO CARRY THE CANE OR WALKING STICK

There are numerous methods to carry the cane or walking stick but the following are the most common ways people walk with a cane. 1. Standing in a natural stance with the hook of the cane to the rear. 2. Natural stance with the hook of the cane to the front.

1.

2.

3. Two Hand Palms Down Grip: Your hands are evenly placed on the Hanbo, cane or walking stick with your arms shoulder width apart.

4. Two-Hand Carry One Palm Up and One Palm Down Grip: (1) Your hands are evenly placed on the Hanbo, cane or walking stick shoulder width apart with one of your hands palm down and your other hand palm down. (2) Two-Hand Carry one palm up and one palm down middle position Grip/Carry

5. One Hand Carry Grip:
   Grasp the Hanbo about three
   Or four inches from end.

6. Two-Hand Sword Grip:
   Grasp the Hanbo using
   both hands at the grip end
   but be sure the hands are not
   touching each other.

7. One Hand Reverse Carry Grip: Grasp the stick about five inches from the end.

8. Two Hand Reverse Carry Grip Grasp the stick with both hands in the reverse grip position.

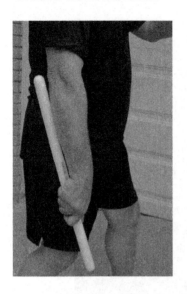
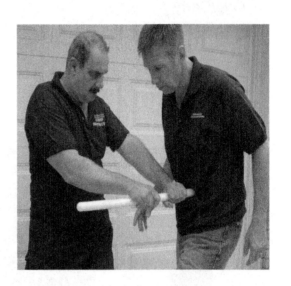

9. Two-Hand Reverse Grip using the Hanbo: (1) Grasp the Hanbo with a palm up and palm down grip at the end of the staff so that the long portion is pointing downward. (2) Pull and push upward into the groin area.

1.   2.

CHAPTER 4

BASIC SELF-DEFENSE PRINCIPLES & USE OF FORCE FACTORS

KEYS TO SELF DEFENSE SUCCESS

There are many important factors involved in any self-defense situation. However, the following four areas are the most vital to successful self-defense. Though this information was written for law enforcement officers in mind, the principles remain the same for any successful self-defense course. This information came originally from the Monadnock Defensive tactics system official manual written by Joseph J. Truncale and Terry E. Smith.

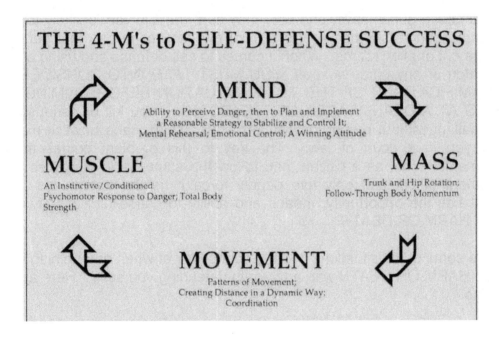

The above illustrates the importance of total effort to achieve success in self-defense. The basic four factors include: MIND-MASS-MOVEMENT-MUSCLE. They represent your total effort. Take away any one of those factors and you reduce your total effort by 25% and risk failure. Take away any two of the above and you reduce your total effort by 50% and failure becomes a possibility. Take away any three of the above and your reduce your total effort by 75% and failure is almost guaranteed. Remember to use your MIND, MASS, MOVEMENT AND MUSCLE to ensure a TOTAL EFFORT.

USE OF FORCE FACTORS IN SELF-DEFENSE

There has been some controversy concerning the "One Punch Kill" theory of Karate. It is my personal view that this myth in karate was adopted from the Japanese sword arts such as Kenjutsu. Indeed, the one cut kill was what the Samurai worked toward in his Kenjutsu training. This does not mean that one cannot kill with just one powerful blow using just the body's own natural weapons. However, anyone who has been involved in full contact fighting realizes that it is not always easy to knock someone out with only one punch. Even the strongest punchers usually require a combination of strikes before knocking their opponents out. I believe the early masters of karate did strive to develop the most powerful strikes, which in theory could kill with one strike. However, the missing part of this equation is target selection on the human body. Indeed, one can knock out and even kill with just one punch or strike. It is all based on aiming at the most vulnerable parts of the body, which will cause the most damage.

For example, a punch at my shoulder may hurt, but it is very unlikely to kill me. If the same punch is aimed at the side of my neck or throat, that punch may knock me out or even kill me. When it comes to self-defense and using a Hanbo, cane, baton or any other weapon, YOU MUST TAKE INTO CONSIDERATION THE RAMIFICATIONS OF THE TOTAL SITUATION BEFORE AIMING YOUR STRIKES AT A DEADLY AREA OF THE BODY. If you kill or seriously injure your assailant without proper justification, your Hanbo, cane or stick may work against you in a court of law. The key to this problem comes from law enforcement. You, as a citizen, can follow the same basic principles. A law enforcement officer can only use deadly force if he/she determines that the assailant has the opportunity, means and ability to cause him or her, GREAT BODILY HARM OR DEATH.

What are some of the situations that the courts look at when determining GREAT BODILY HARM OR DEATH was a factor in defending yourself? Here are a few examples.

1. An attacker has a weapon and the defender has no weapon.
2. The attacker is much larger than the defender.
3. There are multiple attackers against the defender.
4. There was no opportunity to escape the situation.
5. The attacker was attempting to seriously hurt another person in the area.
6. There were no other options available for the defender.
7. The defender seriously felt the attacker's action put him/her in danger of "Great bodily harm or death." This could also include others in the area.
8. The attacker is attempting to choke you by any means and you feared for your life.

9. The attacker is trained in the fighting arts, which could be boxing, kickboxing, karate, jujitsu, mixed martial arts, and any other combat art.
10. The attacker is much younger than the victim.
11. The victim (defender) is a senior citizen and the attacker is young.
12. The victim (defender) is handicapped in some way when attacked.

There may be other factors, but the above can serve as a basic guide.
Check with your local law enforcement agency, state and federal laws concerning the use of force for self-defense.

CHAPTER 5

TARGET AREAS AND YOUR BODY'S NATURAL WEAPONS FOR SELF-DEFENSE

TARGET AREAS:

There are numerous areas of the body that are vulnerable to strikes, locks and control holds. In combatives, the philosophy is to focus on areas of the body that will stop the assailant as quickly as possible. In situations where we are dealing with possible great bodily harm and/or deadly force attacks, we should aim for the most vulnerable areas of the body. Using the Hanbo, cane, walking stick or baton gives the defender other options to stop an attacker. For example, striking an attacker's arms with a staff may be all that is needed to stop the assailant from further assaults. However, if the assailant has a weapon, you may have to focus your strikes to more vulnerable areas of the body such as the throat, eyes, neck, groin and head. Each situation or incident must be judged from the totality of circumstances.

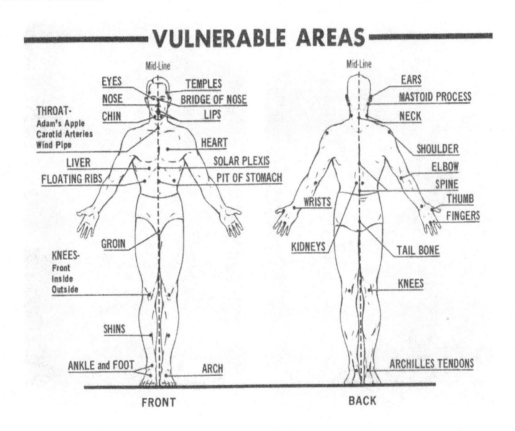

YOUR NATURAL BODY WEAPONS

Even though this is a book on how to use the Hanbo, cane, walking stick and baton, it is also important to understand your body's natural weapons. Though humans are no match for the natural body weapons of most predator animals; nevertheless, we possess numerous weapons on our body to defend ourselves. All it takes is training in these natural body tools. Also, we have the most dangerous weapon, that being the mind. The ability to think, reason, create, design and plan makes humans the most dangerous animal on earth. Besides the mind, the following are the natural weapons we all possess and with training, they can be highly effective self-defense tools. NOTE: Most of these are automatically part of the Pro-Systems Combatives (PSC) system warm up routines.

UPPER BODY WEAPONS: The following seven basic weapons can be employed in hundreds of different ways and angles in combative situations.

1. Forehead: Can be used in very close quarter situations to smash a face.
2. Elbows and Forearms: Another close quarter weapon that can be used in a wide variety of ways to defend yourself.
3. Edge of Hand: One of the most effective self-defense tools of the body.
4. Palm of Hand: Great and effective tool that can be used for self-defense.
5. Fingers: The fingers can poke, jab and thrust into soft body tissues such as the eyes.
6. Fist: Though it takes more training to be good at punching; nevertheless, the fist can be a very powerful tool for self-defense. Note: The back fist strike can also be employed for self-defense but it usually is not as effective as the punch with the fist.
7. Hammer Fist: This is a variation of the edge of hand, but makes the hand stronger when making a fist to strike with the edge portion of the hand.

LOWER BODY WEAPONS:

1. Knees: Can be used to smash into the groin, bladder, and thighs of the attacker.
2. Ball of Foot: Can be used to strike the groin, thighs and other areas of the body.
3. Edge of Foot: Can be used to strike the ankles, kneels, thighs, groin and other areas of the body.
4. Heel of Foot: Can be used to smash the foot, toes, shin, groin, head, neck and other areas of the body.

CHAPTER 6

BASIC HANBO, CANE, STICK BLOCKING TECHNIQUES

It is essential to learn strong blocking techniques in real life self-defense. The reason is simple. If you block hard enough with the Hanbo, cane, walking stick or baton that may stop the assailant from further action against you. Even in unarmed tactics, if you understand the principles of powerful blocking, you may be able to end the confrontation without using further strikes.

There are numerous blocking techniques in Hanbo Jutsu, but they all fall under five basic attacking angles. They are:

1. **High Angle Attacks**: These are strikes usually coming to your head and face area. They can be done downward or straight on from your neck upward.

2. **Low Angle Attacks:** These strikes come either straight in or in an upward angle toward your legs and groin area.

3. **Left Side Angle Attacks:** These strikes come from your left side and include such things as hook punches, roundhouse kicks and swinging attacks to your left side area.

4. **Right Side Angle Attacks:** These strikes come from your right side and include such things as hook punches, roundhouse kicks and swinging attacks to your right side.

5. **Middle Angle Attacks:** These are strikes usually coming forward toward the middle portion of your body from the waist to chest areas.

BLOCKING TECHNIQUES USING THE NIGHT STICK OR POLICE BATON:

The Club: (24 to 36 inches) relates to any straight police baton or riot stick, which could also include a cane, a walking stick, a broom, a mop, a Hanbo or any other stick like object that could be used for self-defense in emergency situations. The club techniques can also relate to almost any staff or sword like object such as the Japanese Hanbo, Katana or Wakizashi.

Basic One Hand Blocks:

One hand blocks are not as effective as two-hand blocking techniques, but they can be used in some counter-attack situations where the attacker threw a punch or attempted to grab you. Note: Even though these blocks are shown blocking another stick, these blocks can be used against punches and other types of attacks.

High Block   1   2

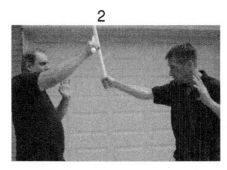

Low Block   1   2

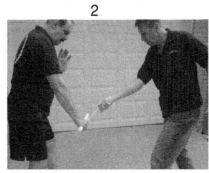

Right Side Block   Left Side Block
1   2

Basic Two-Hand Blocks:

Two-hand blocks are the strongest and most effective techniques because they are most likely to stop an attacker from further assaults on you. Important note: Even though the photographs show blocking with attacks from another stick, these blocks can be used against punching or other types of attacks.

1
High Block

2
Low Block

3
Left Side Block

4
Right Side Block

Blocks Using Two-Hand Reverse Grip:

1 High Block

2 Low Block

3 Left Side (Inside) Block

4 Right Side (Outside) Block

Middle Block using the reverse grip:

TWO HAND MIDDLE GRIP BLOCKING TECHNIQUES:

You can use either the both palms down two-hand grip or the one palm up and one palm down two-hand grip when practicing these blocks:

    A. High Block: Using both hands, thrust the middle portion of the Hanbo, cane or stick upward over your head in a horizontal position to block a high attack.

    B. Low Block: Using both hands, thrust the middle portion of the Hanbo, cane or stick downward below your groin area. Bend your legs but keep your back straight when performing this block.

    C. Right Side Block: Using both hands, thrust the middle portion of the Hanbo, cane or stick to your right side in a VERTICAL position.

    D. Left Side Block: Using both hands, thrust the middle portion of the Hanbo, cane or walking stick to your left side in a VERTICAL position.

 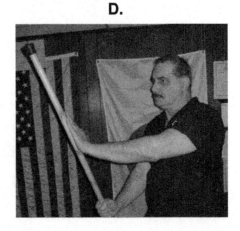

E. Middle Block: Using both hands, thrust the middle portion of the Hanbo, cane or stick toward the middle of your body. The Hanbo, cane, stick can be thrust forward either horizontal or at a 45 degree angle. Note: You can use either the palm up/palm down grip or both palms down grip.

TWO-HAND SWORD GRIP BLOCKING TECHNIQUES:

A. HIGH RIGHT SIDE PUNCH OR GRAB ATTACK COUNTER: Holding the Hanbo, walking stick/cane on one end with the palms facing each other. Swing the walking stick/cane toward your left side blocking a right punch or grabbing attack. This block can be used to counter a high right side grab or strike.

B. **HIGH LEFT SIDE PUNCH OR GRAB ATTACK COUNTER:** Holding the Hanbo, walking stick/cane on one end with the palms facing each other, swing the walking stick/cane toward your right side. This block can be used to counter a left hand punching or kicking attack.

C. **BLOCKING A KICK WITH THE SWORD GRIP:** As the attacker throws a front kick, swing the Hanbo, walking stick/cane in a downward circle striking the attacker's kicking leg.

CHAPTER 7

BASIC STRIKING TECHNIQUES USING THE HANBO, CANE, STICK

Hanbo-Jutsu is an art that uses the entire stick in combat. The sword grip is one of the most effective ways to use the Hanbo, cane, walking stick and baton. This chapter will cover using the stick in the sword grip. It is important to use your whole body when delivering any type of strike with the Hanbo, cane, walking stick or baton.

Forward Thrust strike: Using the Two-hand sword grip, thrust the tip of the Hanbo (cane, walking stick or baton) forward, using your whole body for power.

1.

2.

Forward Cross Body Strike: Using the sword grip, swing the Hanbo (cane, walking stick or baton) forward across your body.

1.

2.

Downward Strike from the Jodan (overhead) position: Using the sword grip, swing the Hanbo (cane, walking stick, baton) downward in a straight line.

1.

2.

Right Side (Hasso position) downward strike: Using the sword grip, swing the Hanbo (cane, walking stick, baton) in a downward angle toward the middle of your body.

1.

2.

Left Side (Hasso position) downward strike: Using the sword grip, swing the Hanbo, (cane, walking stick, baton) in a downward angle toward the middle of your body.

1

2

OVERHEAD FULL CIRCLE SWING USING THE WALKING STICK:
Swing the Hanbo, cane or stick over your head in a clockwise motion. If you are right-handed or swing the stick counter clockwise over your head if you are left-handed.

1.

2.

3.

Forward and Reverse Swing with Hooked cane:

Note: Swings with a cane can be done either hook up or hook down. Swing the cane forward across your body until your hand touches the side of your body. Reverse the same movement across your body to complete a FORWARD AND REVERSE SWING with the cane.

1.

2.

3.

One-Hand Baton Swing Strikes:

Upward Swing Strike: (1) Swing the baton in an upward angle toward the groin.
Downward Swing Strike: (2) Swing the baton from the overhead position downward.

Upward Swing Strike 1   2 Downward Swing Strike   3

Forward Swing Strike: (1-2) Swing the baton across your body in a horizontal manner ending with your baton hand touching your opposite side.

1   2

Reverse Swing Strike: (1-2) upon completing the forward swing strike, rotate your hips as you perform a reverse swing strike with the baton.

1   2

Two-Hand Baton Long Position Grip Jabs/Thrusts: The main difference between a Jab and a Thrusting movement is the Jab is a quick in and out move where the Thrust is a full power technique, burying the strike into the attacker. You should practice both the Jab and Thrust techniques.

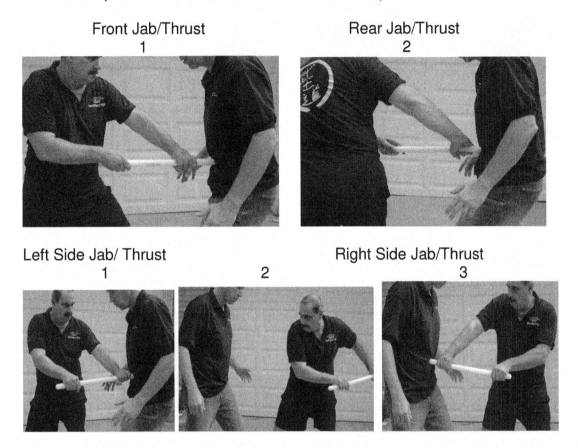

Two-Hand Baton Left & Right Hook Strikes: The Hook Strike is done with the end portions of the baton. The motion is the same as if you were throwing a left and right hook punches with your hands, in that you rotate the waist area when delivering these strikes.

1   Left Side Middle Strike   2   Right Side Middle Strike

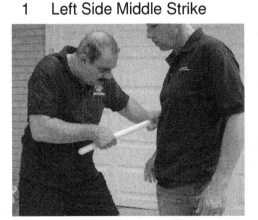 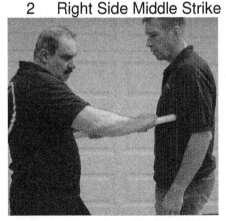

3   Left Side Low Strike

4   Right Side Low Strike

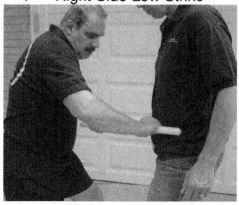

Two-Hand Sword Grip Strikes: The same motion using the one-hand swing strikes are used when performing the Two-Hand Sword Grip. The big difference is that the two-hand sword grip you can strike much harder and use your whole body when delivering the strikes.

1   Upward Strike into Groin   2

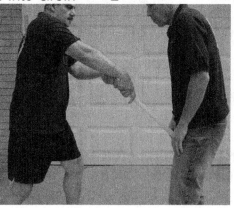

3   Downward Strike to Shoulders   4

5   Forward Cross Body Strike   6

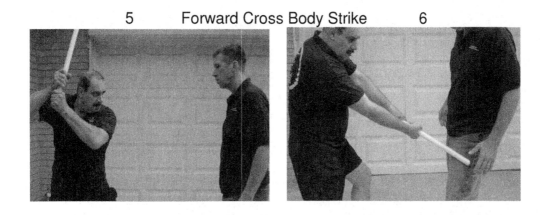

7   Reverse Cross Body Strike   8

Reverse Grip One-Hand Jabs: Doing strikes from the one-hand reverse position is not as effective as using a two-hand grip. However, there are situations where it can be used, such as when you are blocking or grabbing with the opposite (non-baton holding) hand.

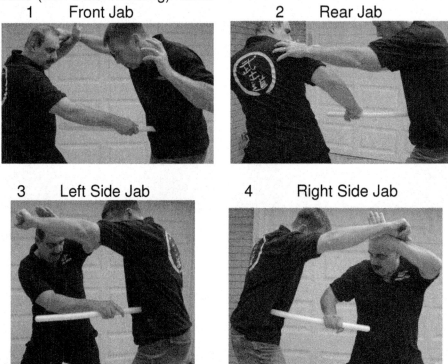

1 Front Jab 2 Rear Jab 3 Left Side Jab 4 Right Side Jab

Reverse Grip Two-Hand Thrusts: Use your whole body when doing the two-hand reverse grip thrusts.

1 Front Thrust 2 Rear Thrust 3

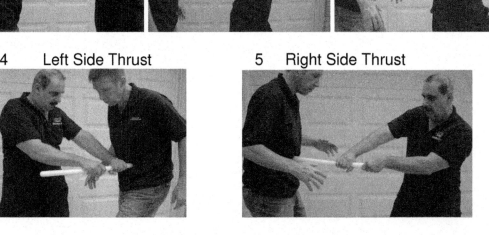

4 Left Side Thrust 5 Right Side Thrust

Two-Hand Reverse Grip Swing Strikes: These can be powerful strikes when using the whole body in delivering these swing strikes.

1 Upward Swing Strike 2

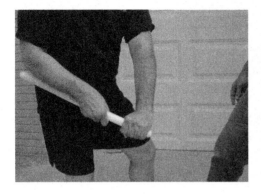 

3 Downward Swing Strike 4

5 Forward Swing Strike 6

7　　　Reverse Swing Strike　　8

CHAPTER 8
HANBO-JUTSU (CANE/NIGHT STICK)
CONTROL AND TAKEDOWN TECHNIQUES

This chapter will cover some basic control and takedown techniques that can be done with the Hanbo, cane, walking stick or police baton. It is important to note that control techniques using the stick or baton of 24 to 26 inches works better than a longer stick in most cases. Keep in mind that it is important to neutralize the subject's ability to strike you before attempting a control technique. This is why it is suggested that these control techniques should first begin with a strong block and/or strike to successfully complete the movements.

Basic Arm Lock using the staff or baton:

Place the long portion of the stick between the subject's upper arm and body just above the triceps. (1) Grasp the long portion of the baton with your left hand while keeping the grip portion at the subject's wrist area with your thumb on the subject's wrist. (2) Pull the long portion of the baton which will bend the subject's arm behind his back. (Note: You can either pull the subject so you end up behind him or you can step behind him as you apply the hold) (3-4) Complete the hold by maintaining control of the baton, and place your hand on the subject's arm/shoulder area. (Note: In most police control techniques the subject is taken to the ground).

Long Position Grip Locks and Takedowns: Arm Locks & Arm Bars

1   2   3   4.

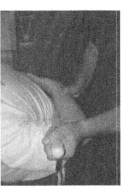
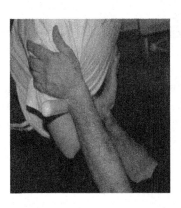

Arm Bar Takedown: Grasp the subject's wrist and pull the arm straight as you place the long portion of the baton just above the elbow joint area. Push down on the baton as you pull up on the wrist area, forcing the subject to the ground.

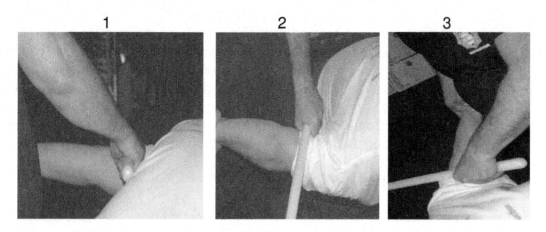

Reverse Grip Arm Locks and Takedowns: (1) Using the Reverse grip, place the grip portion of the baton under the subject's arm just above the elbow area. (2) Grasp the short portion of the baton with your opposite hand. (3) Pull down on the short portion, bending the subject's as you step behind him. (4) Complete the arm-lock. Note: You can take the subject to the ground or place him against a solid object.
Strong Side Arm-Lock

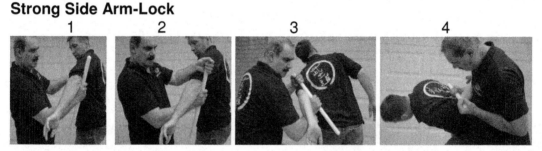

Support Side Arm-Lock (CLAMP) (1) Grasp the subject's wrist with your non-baton holding hand. (2) Pull the subject's arm out as you place the baton arm over the subject's shoulder area. (3) Rotate the baton and place the grip portion over your wrist/forearm area to complete the arm lock.

Reverse Grip X Lock Takedowns:
Front X Lock Takedown: The X lock is an effective takedown technique when a subject's hand(s) are placed on you in some way. It could be a lapel grab or a hand-choke attack. Note: Keep in mind that you may have to strike the subject first in order to neutralize him before attempting any control or takedown technique. (1) Attacker grabs your collar. (2) Rotate your baton around the attacker's arm, placing the long portion on his forearm area. (3) Place your non-baton holding hand on the opposite end of the baton forming an X. (4) Use both of your hands in a downward motion rotating the baton, forcing the subject to the ground.

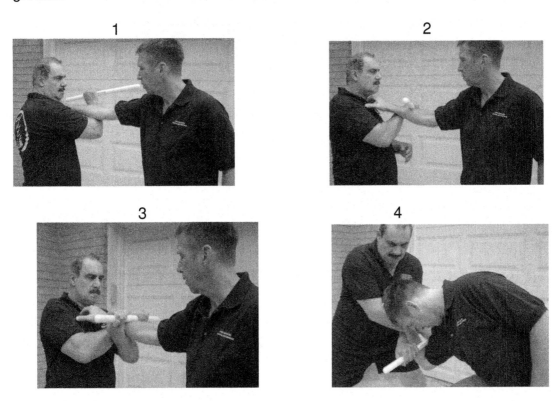

Rear X Lock Takedown: (1) Place the long portion on the subject's forearm area. (2) Grasp the opposite end of the baton with your non-baton hand. (3) Apply pressure downward taking subject to the ground.

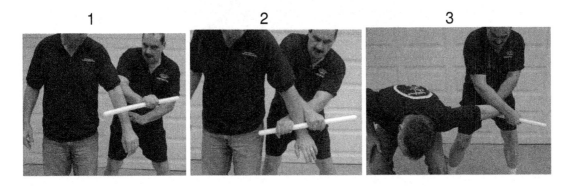

Reverse Grip Arm-Bar Takedown: Grasp the subject's wrist with your non-baton holding hand, twisting the subject's wrist so the palm of his hand is pointing upward. Place the grip portion of the baton just above the subject's wrist area and apply pressure downward as you pull up on the subject's wrist. Lock up the subject on the ground.

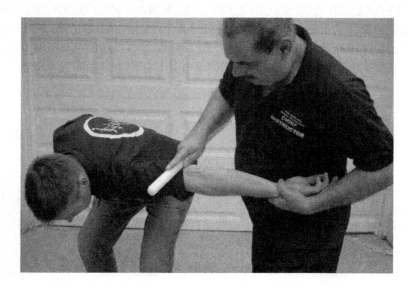

GROUND LOCK UP POSITION FOR ALL TAKEDOWNS:

Notice: The end ground lock up position for all take down techniques is the same, which is placing one knee on the upper shoulder area and the other knee on the ground next to the subject's shoulder facing toward the subject's feet. Squeeze your legs together to lock the shoulder area.

Ground Lock Up Position for all take down techniques:

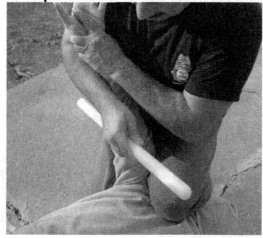

CHAPTER 9

PUNCHING ATTACK COUNTERS

(HANBO, WALKING STICK/CANE SELF-DEFENSE APPLICATIONS)

The fact is there are thousands of self-defense techniques and variations that can be done using the Hanbo, cane and walking stick as a defense tool. It would take several volumes to show even a fraction of the self-defense applications. This manual will show the most common types of assaults and how to counter them using the Hanbo, walking stick or cane. A book or video can only point the way, but if you desire to seek out further training in the use of the Hanbo, cane and/or walking stick, there are numerous self-defense schools who offer this training. The wide world web has numerous resources relating to the Hanbo, cane and walking stick for self-defense. Keep in mind, it is not the number of techniques you learn, but how effective you can be with a few basic techniques that can be applied in multiple self-defense situations.

PUNCHING ATTACK COUNTERS:

1. **Left Punch Attack Counter:** Using the two-hand middle grip thrust the Hanbo cane/walking stick in a vertical position toward the attacker's left punching arm.
   Counter immediately by rotating the cane upward into your attacker's neck.
   Note: Use multiple strikes if needed to stop the attacker from further assaults on you.

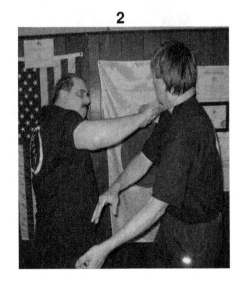

2. **Right Round House Punch Attack Counter**: Using the two-hand middle grip, thrust the cane or walking stick in a vertical position toward the attacker's right punching arm.   Counter by rotating the Hanbo, walking stick or cane downward into the side of the attacker's neck or into the collarbone area. Note: Use multiple strikes if needed to stop the attacker from further assaults on you.

1

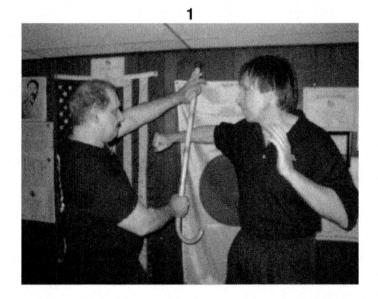

2

3. **Right High Punch Attack Counter:** Using the two-hand middle grip, thrust the cane or walking stick upward blocking the punch. Counter immediately by rotating the walking stick or cane, forward toward the attacker's collarbone and neck area. Note: Use multiple strikes if needed stop the attacker from further assaults on you.

1

2

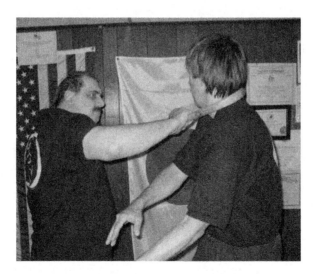

CHAPTER 10

KICKING ATTACK COUNTERS:

(Hanbo, WALKING STICK/CANE SELF-DEFENSE APPLICATIONS)

Front Kick Counter: Drive the middle portion of the Hanbo, walking stick or cane downward stopping the attacker's front kick. Immediately counter with a strike to the attacker's head with the hook or grip portion. Note: You can use numerous strikes as counters once you have blocked the kick.

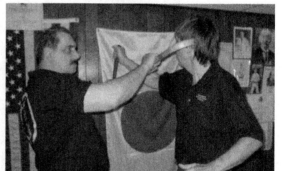

Round Kick Counter: Drive the middle portion of the Hanbo, walking stick or cane in a vertical position blocking the round kick. Immediately counter with a strike to the attacker's neck area with the hook or grip portion of the cane or walking stick.
NOTE: You can use numerous strikes as counters once you have blocked the kick.

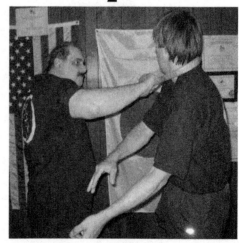

Front Kick Counter using the Sword Grip: Using the sword grip on the Hanbo, cane, walking stick or baton, swing in a downward angle aiming for the kicking leg. You can follow up with various strikes if needed to stop further attacks from the assailant. Notice the block is done with a straight staff and the counter strike is done with a hooked cane. This shows the relationship between the Hanbo, cane, walking stick and baton when used for self-defense.

1.

2.

Chapter 11

CHOKE ATTACK COUNTERS:

(HANBO, WALKING STICK/CANE SELF-DEFENSE APPLICATIONS)

Whenever someone attempts to choke you, whether it is with their hands, arms or an object, you must react immediately and quickly. This can be considered a deadly force attack because it is possible the attack could cause death or great bodily harm.

Front Hand Choke Defense:
1. Attacker begins to choke you with his hands.
2. Using the two-hand grip drive the Hanbo, walking stick or cane upward into the attacker's arms.

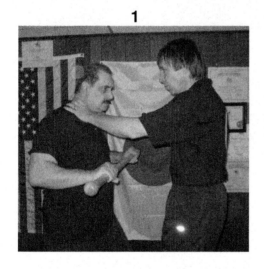

3. Once the choke hold is broken, drive the tip of the Hanbo, walking stick or cane forward into the attacker's head.

Rear Hand Choke Defense:

1. Attacker begins to choke you with his hands.
2. Place the Long Portion of the Hanbo, cane or walking stick between the attacker's legs.
3. Drive the Long Portion of the Hanbo, walking stick or cane upward into the attacker's groin.

Rear Arm Choke Defense:

1. Attacker places his arm around throat.
2. Immediately use your hand to pull the attacker's arm down as you tuck your chin into the attacker's arm. At the same time,
3. drive the Hanbo, cane/walking stick upward into the attacker's groin area.

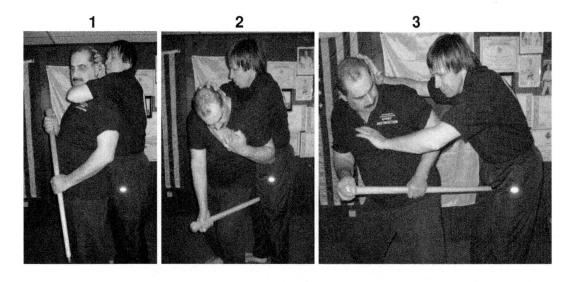

CHAPTER 12

STICK AND WRIST GRAB COUNTERS:
(Hanbo, cane and walking stick self-defense applications)

1. Two-Hand Hanbo, Cane/Walking Stick Grab Counter:
1. Attacker has grabbed your cane in the middle with two hands.
2. Rotate the cane or walking stick in a clockwise circle breaking the attacker's grip on your cane or walking stick.

 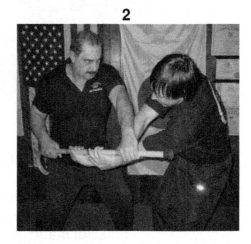

3. With your right hand drive the hook or grip portion forward into the head or neck area to stop his attack. NOTE: A HANBO, CANE OR WALKING STICK CAN BE USED IN ALL OF THESE SELF-DEFENSE TECHNIQUES.

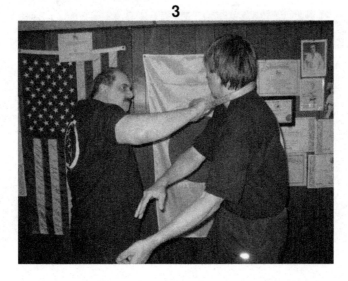

2. Attacker Grabs Your Wrist With Both of His Hands.

1. Attacker grabs your wrist with both of his hands. 2. Rotate the Hanbo, walking stick/cane clockwise over the attacker's hands. 3. When the hold is broken, strike the attacker's head.

1

2
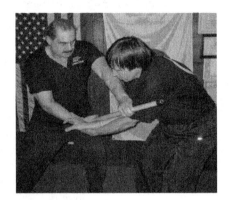

3

CHAPTER 13

BEAR HUG COUNTERS:
(Hanbo, cane and walking stick self-defense applications)

1. **Two Hand Rear Bear Hug Over the Arms Counter:**
   A. Attacker grabs you around your body over your arms.
   B. Move your Hip to the side.
   C. Drive the Shaft (or Long Portion) into attacker's groin area.

2. **Front Bear Hug Around Both Arms Counter:**
   A. Attacker applies a front bear hug around your arms.
   B. Drive the Shaft or Long Portion into attacker's groin.

3. **Front Bear Hug Under the Arms Counter:**

   A. Attacker applies a front bear hug under your arms.
   B. Place the middle portion of the Hanbo, walking stick/cane on the neck area of the attacker and apply pressure downward breaking the hold. You can follow up with strikes if needed.

1

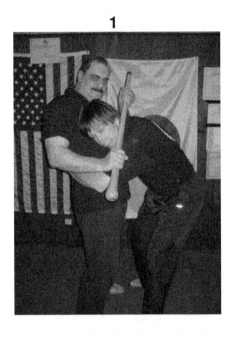

2

CHAPTER 14

KNIFE ATTACK COUNTERS:
(Hanbo, cane, walking stick self-defense application)

Defending against someone with a knife is always dangerous and unpredictable. However, the Hanbo, walking stick or cane can provide an effective weapon to defend yourself. It is important to practice these techniques in a safe but realistic manner. Keep in mind that the knife is a deadly weapon and you may be justified in using deadly force to stop your attacker from causing you great bodily harm or death.

1. Attacker thrusts a knife in an upward motion toward your stomach.
    1. Defender performs a two hand low block.
    2. Follow up with an upward two-hand strike into the attacker's throat.

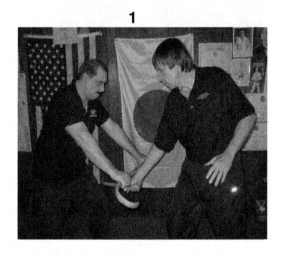

2. Attacker stabs downward using the ice pick grip toward the defender.

1. Defender uses an upward block on the attacker's knife arm.
2. Defender follows up with strike to the attacker's head with the Hanbo, cane, walking stick or cane.

1

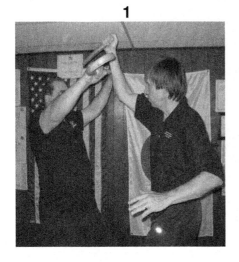

2

3. Knife attacker attempts a forward slashing motion with his knife.
    1. Defender uses a two-hand sword grip and strikes the attacker's knife hand using a downward strike.
    2. Defender follows up with a two-hand sword strike into the attacker's neck.

1

2

4. Knife attacker attempts a forward stabbing motion with his knife.

1. Defender use a two-hand sword grip strike, while pushing down the attacker's knife arm.
2. Defender swings the cane/walking stick in a circle striking the attacker's neck area.

1
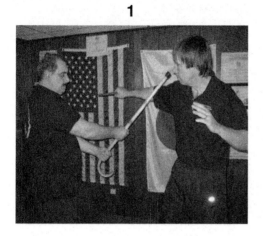

2

3

CONCLUSION

The purpose of this text was to provide a basic introduction to various size staffs from the Hanbo to the traditional straight police baton. This manual is by no means a comprehensive text on the use of the Hanbo, cane or night stick. However, it does provide a basic guide on how to employ the Hanbo, cane, walking stick and standard police baton for self-defense and control.

It is hoped this will spur an interest in the formal staff martial arts, as well as the practical street combatives use of the cane/walking stick and the police baton.

Joseph J. Truncale March 23, 2015 REVISED EDTION.

References and Recommended Material

For this manual and my other publications I have researched, reviewed and investigated numerous sources of information. The following books, manuals, courses and DVDs are highly recommended for those seeking further information on various combative systems, self-defense methods, self-offense publications and other reality based combat systems.

Advanced Krav-Maga by David Kahn
All-In Fighting by W. E. Fairbairn
Advanced PR-24 Baton Techniques by Joseph J. Truncale
American Combat Judo by B. L. Cosneck
Anything Goes: Practical Karate for the streets by Loren W. Christensen
Armor Plated: Defensive Skills for the street DVD set by Mark Hatmaker
Basic Knife Handling & Defense for Law Enforcement Officers by J. Truncale
Basic Manual of Knife Fighting By William L. Cassidy
Black Medicine book series volumes 1 thru 4 by N. Mashiro
Bob Kasper's Individual Close Combat Vol. 1 & 2
Bowie and Big Knife Fighting Systems by Dwight C. McLemore
Boxing by United States Naval Institute
Boxing Mastery by Mark Hatmaker with Doug Werner
Boxing's Dirty Tricks and Outlaw Dirty Punches by Jay C. "Champ" Thomas
Brutal Art of Ripping, Poking and Pressing Points by Loren W. Christensen
Championship Fighting by Jack Dempsey
Championship Street Fighting by Ned Beaumont
Charles Nelson's School of Self-Defense manual
Choke Em Out by Burton Richardson
Close-Quarter Combat by Professor Leonard Holifield
Close Combat Files of Colonel Rex Applegate
Cold Steel by John Styers
Combat Use of the Double-Edged Fighting Knife by Col. Rex Applegate
Combatives by the U.S. Army
Combatives Video Series 1, 2, 3 with Kelly McCann, aka. Jim Grover
Combat Survival: Commando Krav-Maga Vol. 1 Thru 5 entire set by Moni Aizik
Complete Book of Knife Fighting by William L. Cassidy
Complete Krav Maga by Darren Levine and John Whitman
Deadly Karate Blows (The Medical Implications) by Brian Adams
Defending against the Blade video with Peyton Quinn
Defendu by Capt. W. E. Fairbairn
Defensive Shooting for real life Encounters by Ralph Mroz
Defensive Tactics by Loren W. Christensen
Defensive Tactics for Special Operations by Sgt Jim Wagner
Desperate Measures by Michael Vassolo
Dirty Dozen by Larry Jordan
Do or Die by Lt. Col. A. J. Drexel Biddle
Essential Elements of Personal Combat by Prof. Bradley J. Steiner

Extreme Boxing DVD with Mark Hatmaker
Extreme Close Quarter Combat video the Inter. Close Quarter Combat Assoc.
Extreme Joint Locking and Breaking by Loren W. Christensen
Extreme Self-Defense: Counter Terrorist Tactics video with Vince Morris
Far Beyond Defensive Tactics by Loren W. Christensen
Fierce and Female DVD series with Melissa Soalt, aka Dr. Ruthless
F.I.G.H.T. Entire Haganah – Krav Maga DVD series with Mike Lee Kanarek
Fighting Dirty DVD with Loren W. Christensen
Fighting Sword by Dwight C. McLemore
Fighting with Firearms video with Andy Stanford
Flashlight Fighting by Phil Elmore
Get Tough by Capt. W. E. Fairbairn
Guns save Lives by Robert A. Waters
Hand-To-Hand Combat U.S. Army manual
Jim Grover's Situational "Self-Offense" with Kelly McCann
Kamikaze Fighting by Michael Vassolo
KAPAP: Combat Concepts by Avi Nardia and Albert Timen
Kill or Get Killed by Maj. Rex Applegate
Kissaki-Kai Karate-Do video with Vince Morris
Knife Handling & Knife Defense for Law Enforcement Manual by J. Truncale
Krav Maga Video Series with Darren Levine
Krav Maga by David Kahn
Krav Maga: Defend Yourself against Armed Assault by Eyal Yanilov (Imi Sde-Or)
Light Him up DVD with Steve Materkowski
Masters and Styles DVD with Loren Christensen, Mark Hatmaker, Vince Morris
Monadnock Defensive Tactics (MDTS) Official Manual by Truncale and Smith
No Holds Barred Fighting by Mark Hatmaker and Doug Werner
No Second Chance by Bradley J. Steiner
On Combat by Lt. Col. Dave Grossman with Loren Christensen
One against Many DVD with Branimir Tudjan
1,001 Street Fighting Secrets by Sammy Franco
Practical Knife Fighting video Vol. 1, 2 with Datu Kelly S. Worden
Principles of Personal Defense by Jeff Cooper
Raven Method Telescopic Baton by Fernan Vargas
Reality-Based Personal Protection by Jim Wagner
Savage Science of Street Fighting by Ned Beaumont
Savage Strikes by Mark Hatmaker
Scientific self-Defence by W. E. Fairbairn
Strictly Street Stuff by Bill Bryant St.
Tactical Defensive Training for Real-Life Encounters by Ralph Mroz
Tanto Jutsu Official Manual of Bushi Satori Ryu by Joseph J. Truncale
Turning Fear into Power by Bill Kipp
Ultimate Combat Conditioning for the Street Warrior Book by Reeves &Yetman
Use of the Mini Baton Official Course Manual by Joseph J. Truncale
Use of the Monadnock Straight Baton by Joseph J. Truncale
Reverse Grip Baton Official Course Manual by Joseph J. Truncale

Vital Target DVD with Loren W. Christensen
Wakizashi-Jutsu Official course manual of Bushi Satori Ryu by J. Truncale
Warriors Edited by Loren W. Christensen
Way of the Raven: Blade Combatives Vol. 1. By Fernan Vargas
Weapon Retention Official Manual (Pro-Systems) by Joseph J. Truncale
Use of the Cane/Walking Stick for Self-Defense Manual by Joseph J. Truncale

ABOUT THE AUTHOR

Joseph J. Truncale has been involved in the martial arts for more than fifty years. He first took up wrestling and boxing and joined the U.S. Navy in 1959. In 1961, he began his training in Judo and Karate while stationed in Japan aboard the USS Oklahoma City, a guided missile cruiser. He continued his training in Judo and Karate while in the Navy until his honorable discharge in November of 1963. He continued his search for more martial art knowledge, joining a Shotokan Karate club under Mr. Sugiyama, Sensei, (Japan Karate Association) who was the Chief Instructor of the Midwest Shotokan Karate.

In 1965, he joined the Glenview, Il Police Department, and studied Judo at the Glenview Judo club at that time. He also continued his Shotokan Karate training under Mr. Copland, Sensei, who was also a student of Mr. Sugiyama. When Mr. Copland moved from the area, Mr. Truncale continued his training under Mr. Rogers, Sensei, who was also a student of Mr. Sugiyama. At that time, Mr. Truncale also attended numerous police arrest and control seminars becoming a certified instructor in many police tactics systems. He has been involved in the martial arts for more than 40 years, studying many combat and weapons systems under numerous excellent Police and Martial Art Instructors.

He has earned Black Belts in Karate, Godan, Judo, Godan, Jujitsu, Kudan, Soke, Bushi Satori Ryu, and Kobudo, Sandan. Even though Mr. Truncale was inducted in the United States Martial Arts Association Hall of Fame as a Master in 2002, He still considers himself merely a lifetime student of the martial arts. After many Years of Tai Chi training with Laurie Manning, the Ching Ying Tai Chi Kung Fu Association awarded him his official teaching certificate in Tai Chi.

In 1973 Mr. Truncale, Sensei, founded the first Karate club in Glenview at the Glenview Playdium and the Glenview Park District, which was also one of the first Karate clubs on the entire north Shore of Chicago at that time. He also founded the first Jujitsu club in Glenview on the Glenview Naval Air Station around 1980, as well as the first Jujitsu club at the Glencoe Park District around the same time.

Though Mr. Truncale has worked in many areas of law enforcement, his special expertise is in the police defensive tactics and police weapon fields. He has designed numerous police survival courses and has taught police and security officers from all over the world at international seminars. He is a certified International Instructor in the PR-24 Police Baton, the MEB (Monadnock Exp. Straight Baton) program, the Monadnock Defensive Tactics System (MDTS), and the Persuader, Short Stick Baton. He is also a certified Master Instructor in the CLAMP, the GRASP, and OC Spray. He has had the honor to have studied from some of the best minds and most talented martial art and police instructors in the world.

He is the founder (Soke) of BUSHI SATORI RYU, a Jujitsu style that blends the traditional Samurai arts with modern combat methods. The learning of 16 martial art weapons and 12 police weapons are part of the total Bushi Satori Ryu system. He has also created SAMURAI AEROBICS, THE MINI-BATON POLICE TACTICS SYSTEM, THE REVERSE GRIP BATON SYSTEM AND THE PRO-SYSTEMS COMBATIVES (PSC) SYSTEM. He has had more than 2000 papers (articles, essays, reviews and poems) and more than 50 books/manuals published. He also used write several columns in the past and had his own newsletter, THE WARRIOR WAY REVIEWS (WWR) Newsletter for many years.

He is one of the founding directors of The American Society of Law Enforcement Trainers and was on the advisory board of the International Law Enforcement Educators and Trainers Association (ILEETA), The Illinois Police Instructor's Association (IPITA) and the Monadnock Police Training Council.

He is a member of numerous professional associations (ILEETA, ASLET, ITPITA, USJA, USMA, and MPTC). At one time he had taught more than 40 police and citizen self-defense courses. He also taught a college credit course at Oakton Community College for many years. He has taught Jujitsu, Women's Self-Defense and Tai Chi at the Lattof YMCA in Des Plaines, Ill. He is now retired but still teaches seniors Seated Tai-Chi and writes reviews on Amazon.

BOOKS, MANUALS, AND GUIDES
By
Joseph J. TRUNCALE

1. PR-24 Police Baton Techniques: Basic and Advanced Techniques: (Co-author: with Connors Univ. of IL Press)
2. Police Yawara Stick Techniques: (Co-author: with Connors Univ. of IL)
3. Advanced PR-24 Baton Techniques: Monadnock Lifetime Products, Inc.
4. Use of the Straight Baton: Monadnock Lifetime Products, Inc.
5. The Monadnock Defensive Tactics System: (Co-Author Smith) Monadnock
6. The Persuader Baton(Revised original text by Eric Chambers) Monadnock
7. Mechanics of Arrest and Control: For Law Enforcement. Rational Press
8. The Rational Approach to Arrest and Control: Rational Press
9. The Persuader Defense Systems Manual: Pro-Systems Publishing
10. Basic Handbook of Hypnosis for Law Enforcement: Pro-Systems
11. Rational Self-Hypnosis for Police Officers: Pro-Systems
12. Rational Self-Hypnosis for Everyone: Pro-Systems
13. Use of the Key Chain Holder for Self-Defense: (Co-author)
14. The Pro-Systems Official Weapon Retention Manual: Pro-Systems
15. Use of the Pepper Spray for Self-Defense Basic Manual: Pro-Systems
16. The FIST(Fast-Intense-Strong-Techniques)System of Self-Defense: Pro-Sys
17. Season of the Warrior: A Poetic Tribute to Warriors: Author House Pub.

18. A Quick Course Guide to Women's Self-Defense: Pro-Systems
19. A Quick Course Guide to the Use of the Persuader Baton: Pro-Systems
20. A Quick Course Guide to Total Physical Fitness: Pro-Systems
21. Use of the Scientific Method & Pseudoscience: A Quick Course Guide.
22. A Quick Course Guide to Writing for Publication: Pro-Systems
23. A Quick Course Guide to Great Books of Civilization: Pro-Systems
24. A Quick Course Guide to Elements of Officer Survival: Pro-Systems
25. Facts and Fallacies in Police Defensive Tactics Manual: Pro-Systems
26. Truth and Fiction in the Martial Arts and Self-Defense: Pro-Systems
27. Common Myths about Women's Self-Defense: Pro-Systems
28. A Basic Guide to Defending Against Chokes: Pro-Systems
29. A Poetic Tribute to Warriors: Poems and Essay Collection: Pro-Systems
30. A Tribute to Warriors: A Haiku Collection: Pro-Systems
31. Nothing Ever Happens in Glenview: A Poem Collection: Pro-Systems
32. The Bushi Satori Ryu Official Student and Instructor Manual: Pro-Systems
33. The Bushi Satori Ryu Official 15 Weapons Basic Outline Manual: Pro-Sys
34. Knife Handling and Knife Defense Manual: Pro-Systems
35. Use of the Knife for Women's Self-Defense basic manual: Pro-Systems
36. Samurai Aerobics Official Basic Manual: Pro-Systems
37. Basic Use of the Cane Summary Review Manual: Pro-Systems
38. Basic Use of the Cane for Self-Defense Manual: Pro-Systems
39. The Mighty Pen: Your Self-Defense Friend Self-Defense Manual: Pro-Systems

40. The Pro-Systems 3-4 and 6-4 Basic Knife System Manual: Pro-Systems

41. The Bushi Satori Ryu Official Tanto Jutsu Basic Manual: Pro-Systems

42. The Revised (10 Angle System) Law Enforcement Knife Handling and Knife Defense Manual for the official course. Pro-Systems.

43. The Shotokan Karate Self-Defense Manual: Practical Combat Karate.

44. Karate's Multiple Strikes for Self-Defense: Karate's Forgotten Deadly Techniques: Pro-Bushi Publishing (Pro-Systems & Bushi Satori)

45. The Pro-Systems and Bushi Satori Ryu Wakizashi Basic Student Manual

46. Walking With Warriors: The Best of the Street Warrior.

47. Never Trust a Politician: A Critical Review of Politics and Politicians Publisher E-Book Time, LLC March 2008 ISBN NO. 978-1-59824-789-3

48. Baton Reverse Grip System (BRGS) Official Student Manual.

49. Pro-Systems Combatives (PSC) System: Fundamentals and Principles. Official Student Manual. Pro-Bushi Publishing. ISBN Number: 978-0-9815405-1-1

50. Pro-Systems Combatives (PSC) System: Advanced Techniques and Concepts Official Manual. Vol. 2. Pro-Bushi Publishing   ISBN: 978-0- 9815405-0-4

51. Mini-Baton Instructor Course Official Manual Pro-Systems Published in 2004.

52. Martial Arts Myths: Fact and Fallacy about the Martial arts and Law Enforcement: Order from Café Press Publisher. ISBN: 1-892686-11-2

53. Hanbo-Jutsu: Use of the Hanbo, Cane, Walking Stick and Baton for Self-Defense. Pro-Bushi Publishing.

54. The Mighty Pen: Use of the Pen as a Tactical Self-Defense Tool. Pro-Bushi Publishing:

55. Haiku Moments: How to write, read and enjoy Haiku.   Publisher: Publish America. ISBN: 978-1-4512-9364-7 Softcover   978-1-4512-9363-0 Hardcover Order the above book from   www.publishamerica

56. Predator Hunter: A Warrior's Memoir Publisher: Publish America Order from www.publishamerica ISBN: 978-1-4560-1108-6

57. Karate Combatives: Reality-Based Karate for the Street (Vol. 1)   Pro-Bushi Publishing: ISBN: 978-0-9815405-3-5

58. Weapons of Karate Combatives: Karate Combatives (Vol. 2) Pro-Bushi

59. Seated Zen Karate: A Pro-Bushi Basic Manual.

60. Tactical Principles of the most effective combative systems (Revising at this time).

61. A Poetic Tribute to Autumn: The most beautiful time of the year. (PBP)

62. Haiku for special occasions (A Pro-Bushi publication)

63. Short Cat Poems: A poetic tribute to cats (A Pro-Bushi publication)

SPECIAL THANKS

Writing a physical skills text would be impossible without the help of numerous individuals. I humbly thank the following individuals for their assistance and help in putting together the combative series of manuals and course material.

Michael Frey: My long time karate, jujitsu and combatives student and good friend, who is in most of the photographs with me.

Dave Frey, who took most of the excellent photographs for the Combative series of manuals.

Joseph Frey, who took some of the photographs used in this text and in some of my other manuals.

Joseph Mrowiec, my karate and combatives student and good friend, who was also in some of the photographs.

Fernan (Dave) Vargas, whose encouragement and help was invaluable in getting my material published. Without his assistance many of my books and manuals would have been lost to time. Thank you so much my friend.

CPSIA information can be obtained
at www.ICGtesting.com
Printed in the USA
BVOW07s2154040318
509330BV00022B/58/P